I0417928

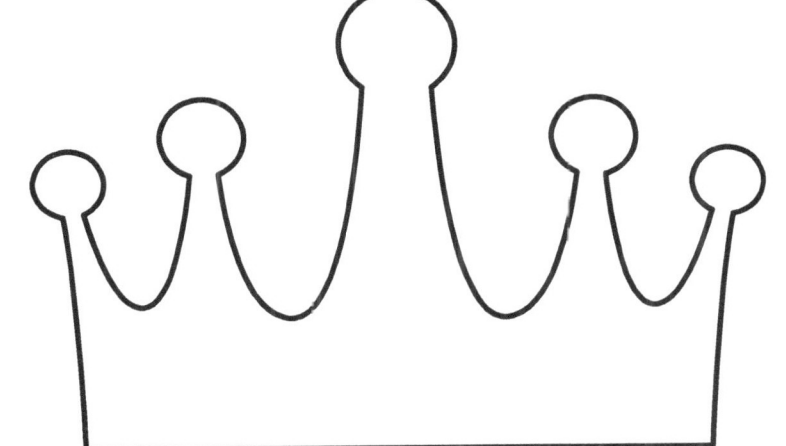

My ALPHABET AFFIRMATIONS

HANDWRITING PRACTICE AND
COLORING WORKBOOK FOR BOYS

Copyright © 2022 by Black Blossom Press

ISBN: 979-8-9868383-0-4

In loving memory of my grandmother, Nana, who filled my life with positive affirmations long before I could place a name to the act.

Her love eternally colored my world for the better.

MY ALPHABET AFFIRMATIONS

What is an affirmation?

An act of saying or showing that something is true.

This book is filled with affirmations to support positive thinking. Saying affirmations help to build habits of positive self thoughts.

This book will introduce your child to positive affirmations in alignment with the alphabet that teach self-love and build confidence to unlock their inner greatness.

At the end of this book, cut out the template to create a list of daily positive affirmations that you and your child can see and say everyday.

We'd love to hear from you!

✉ Email
blackblossompress@gmail.com

◻ Instagram
@blackblossompress

MY ALPHABET AFFIRMATIONS

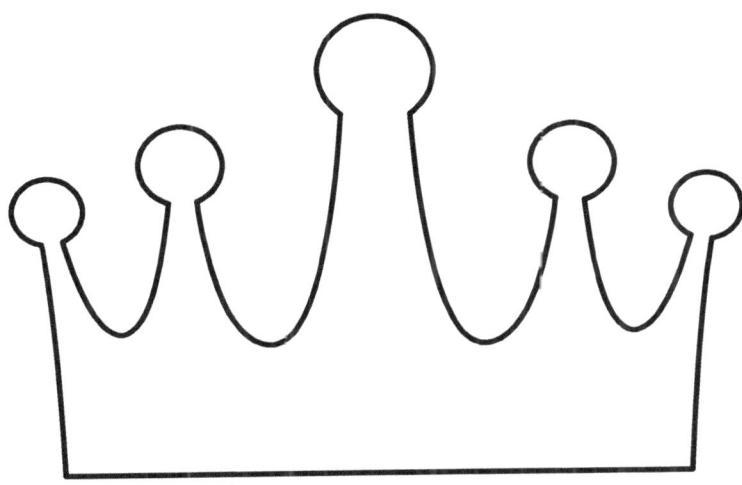

THIS BOOK BELONGS TO:

I CAN ACHIEVE ANYTHING I SET MY MIND TO.

A

Practice writing the affirmation in the lines below.

I can achieve

I can achieve

I can achieve

I can achieve

I can achieve

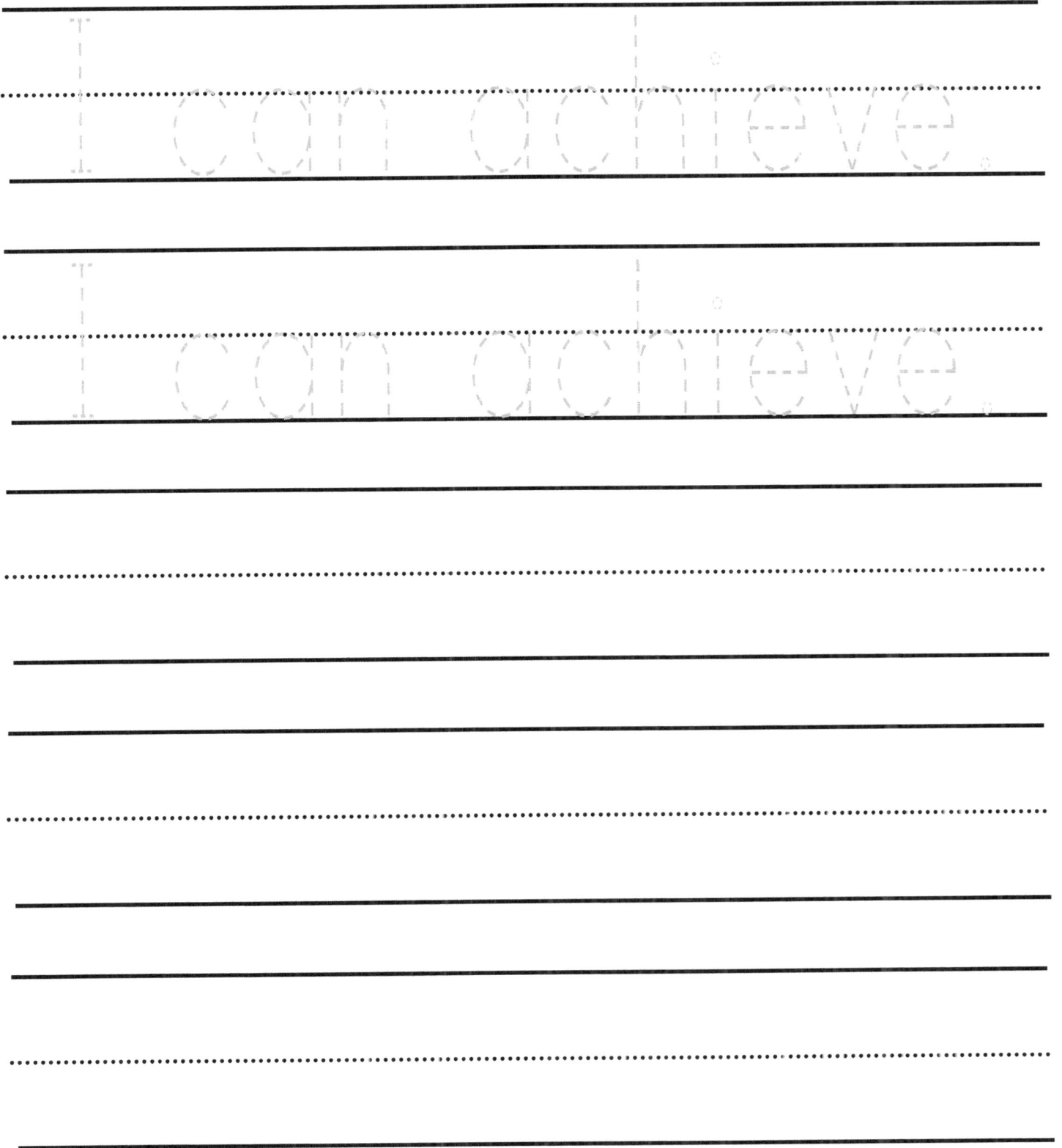

I can achieve.

B Practice writing the affirmation in the lines below.

I am brave.

I am brave.

I am brave.

I am brave.

I am brave

I am brave.

I am brave.

Practice writing the affirmation in the lines below.

I am confident

I am confident

I am confident

I am confident

I am confident

I am confident.

I am confident.

D Practice writing the affirmation in the lines below.

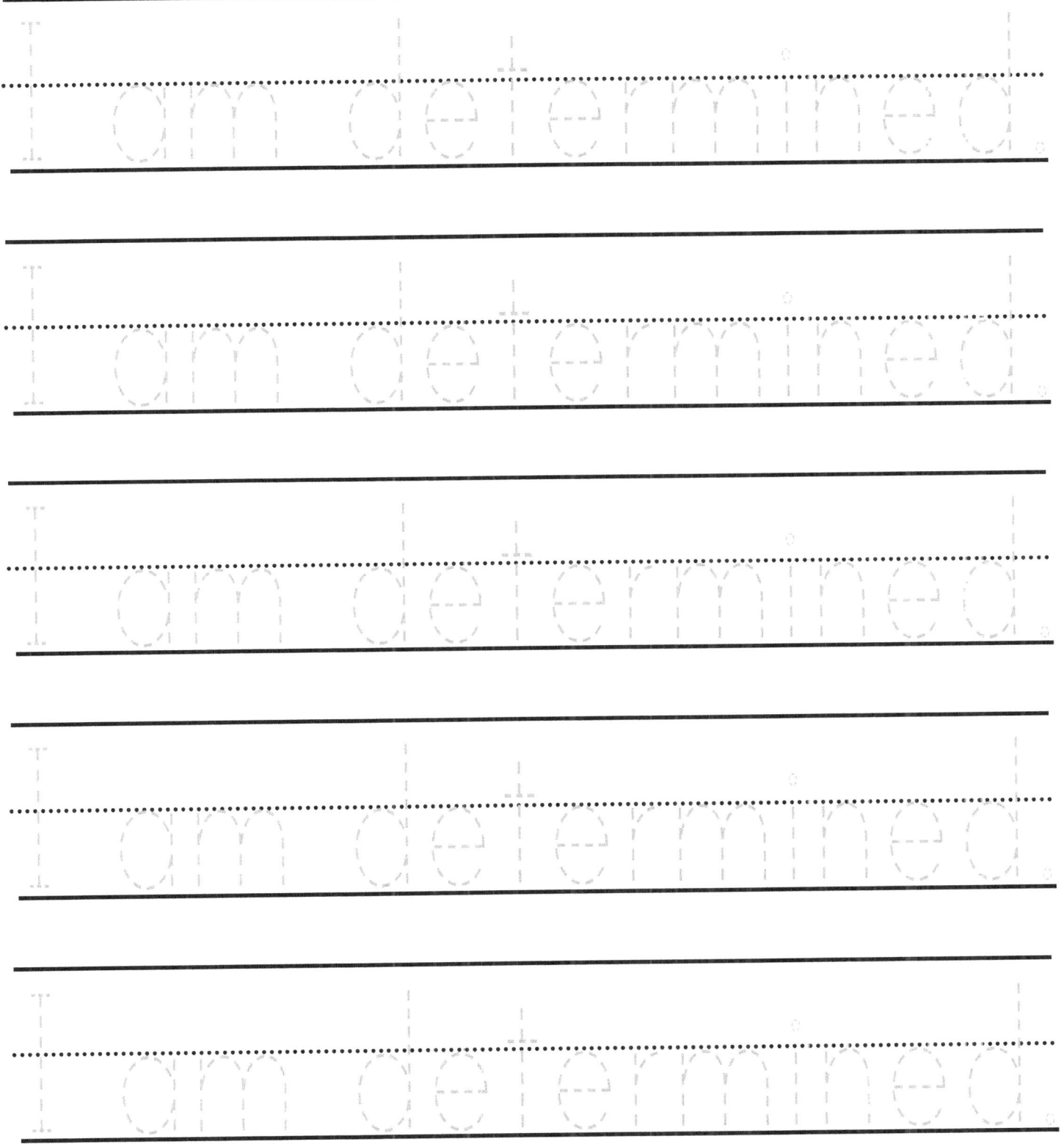

I am determined.

I am determined.

I am determined.

I am determined.

I am determined.

I am determined.

I am determined.

I AM ENOUGH

E

Practice writing the affirmation in the lines below.

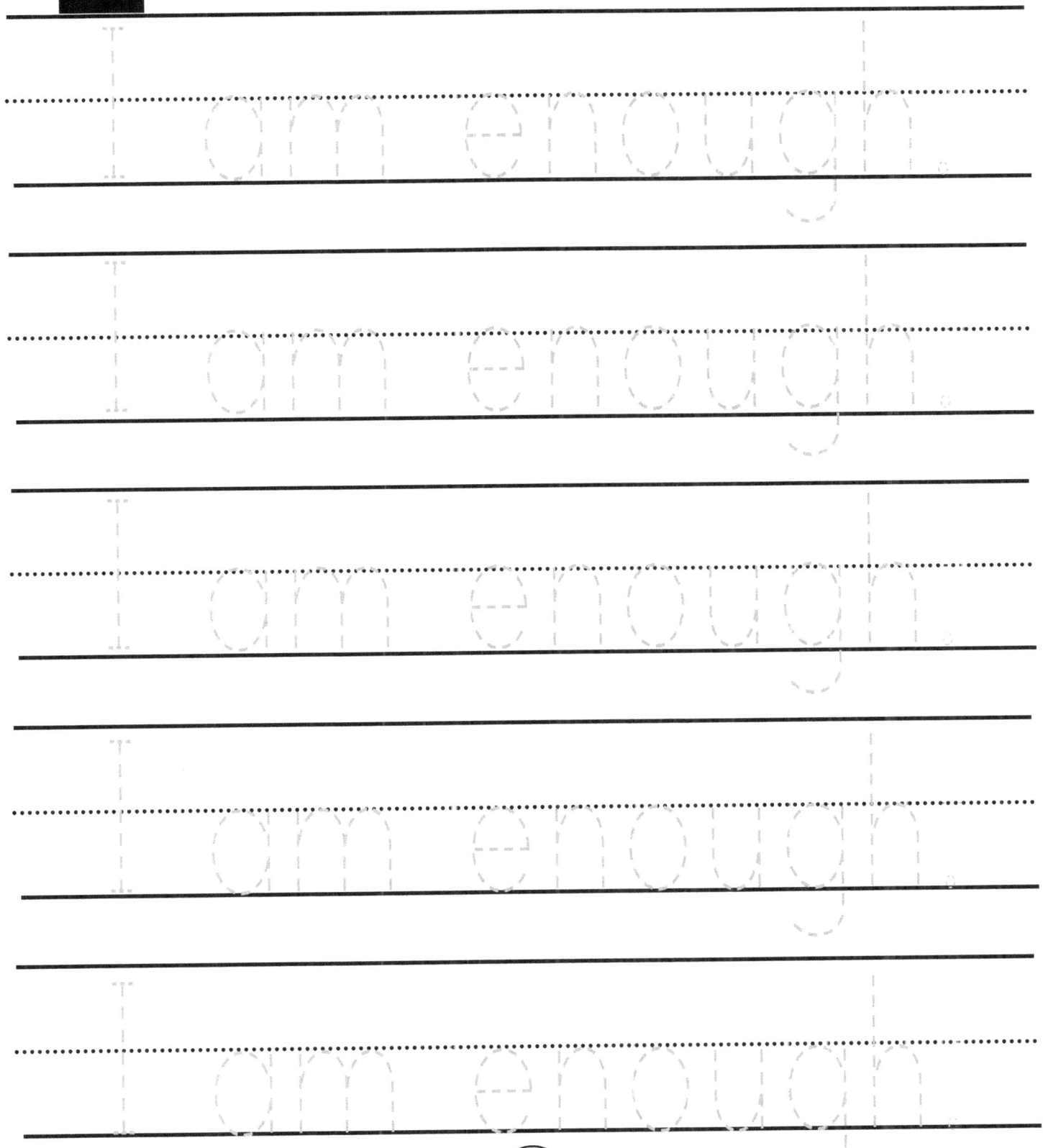

I am enough.

I am enough.

F

Practice writing the affirmation in the lines below.

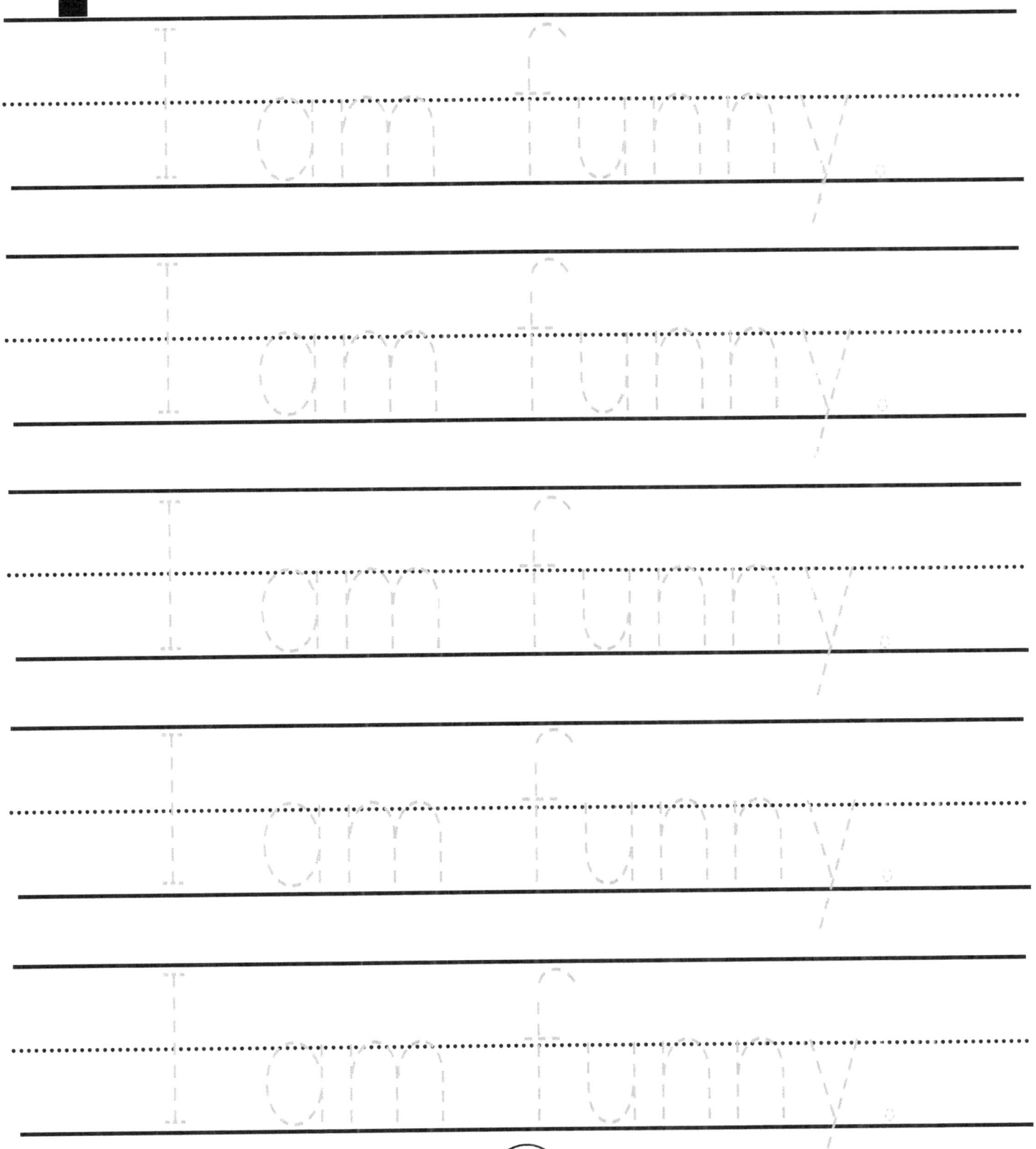

I am funny.

I am funny.

I AM GRATEFUL FOR WHO I AM AND WHAT I HAVE.

G

Practice writing the affirmation in the lines below.

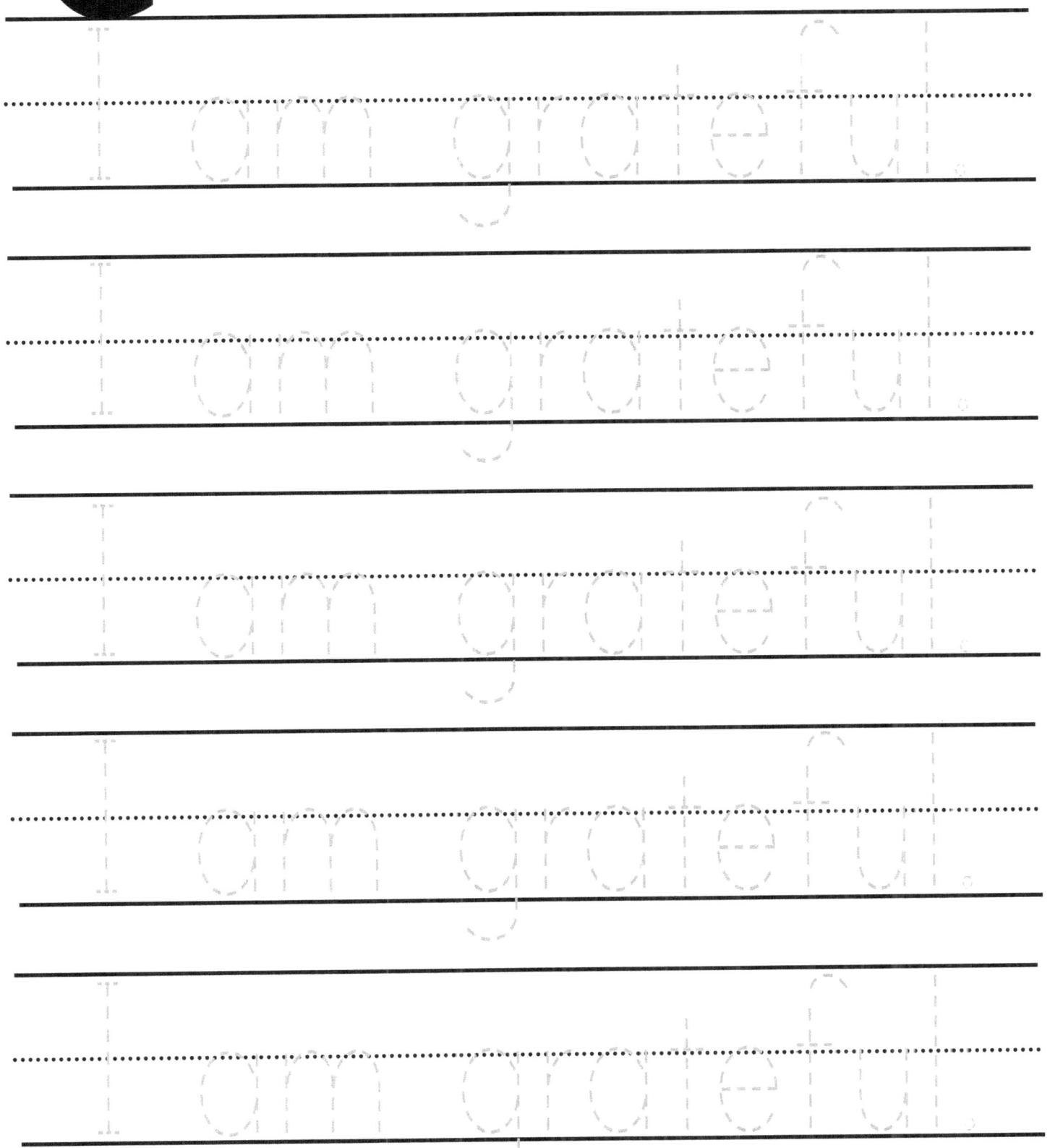

I am grateful.

I am grateful.

Practice writing the affirmation in the lines below.

I am honest.

I am honest.

I am honest.

I am honest.

I am honest.

I am honest.

I am honest.

Practice writing the affirmation in the lines below.

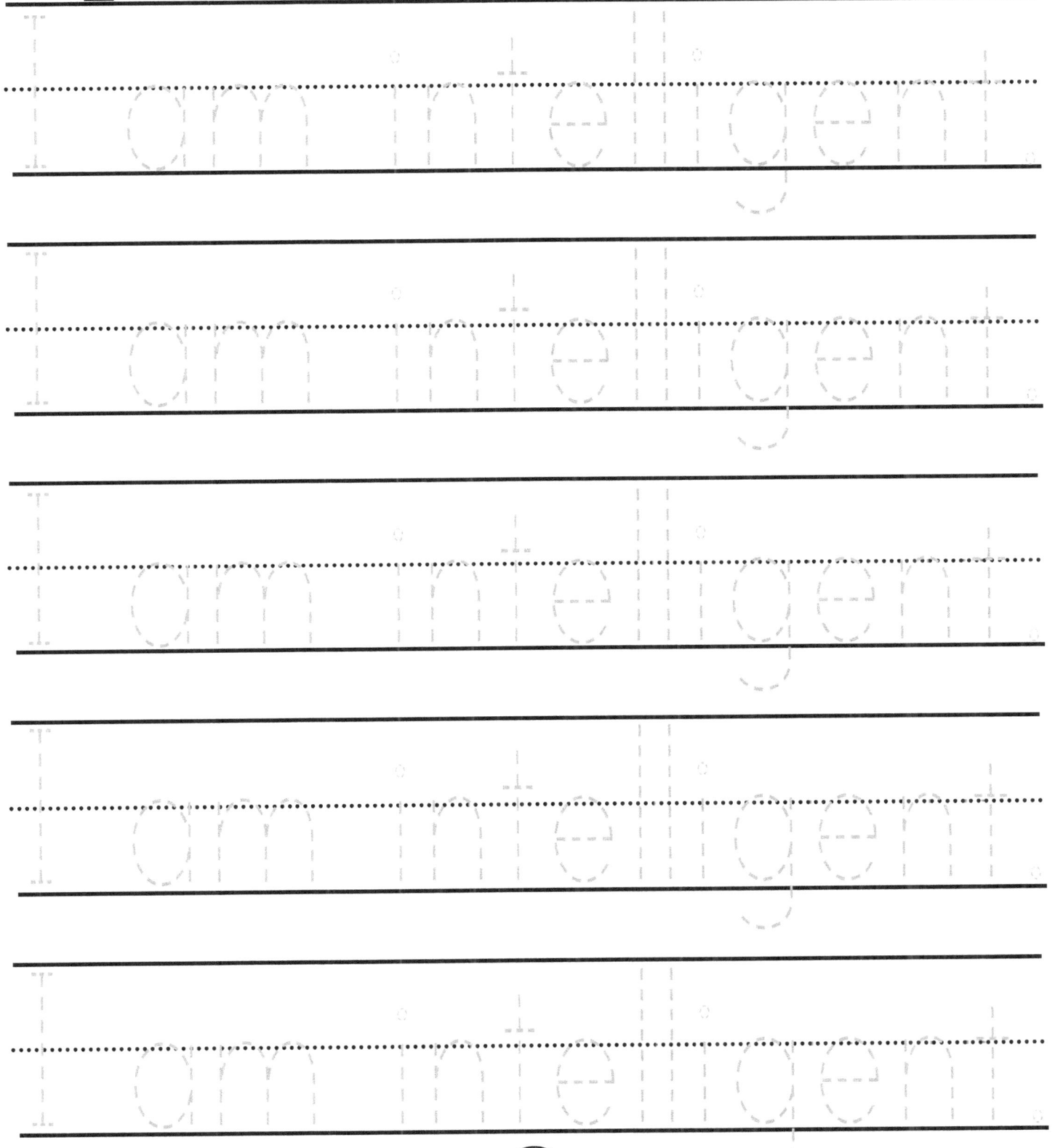

I am intelligent

I am intelligent

I HAVE JOY

J

Practice writing the affirmation in the lines below.

I have joy

I have joy

I have joy

I have joy

I have joy

I have joy.

K

Practice writing the affirmation in the lines below.

I am kind

I am kind

I am kind

I am kind

I am kind

I am kind.

I am kind.

L

Practice writing the affirmation in the lines below.

I am a leader

I am a leader

I am a leader

I am a leader

I am a leader

I am a leader.

I am a leader.

M

Practice writing the affirmation in the lines below.

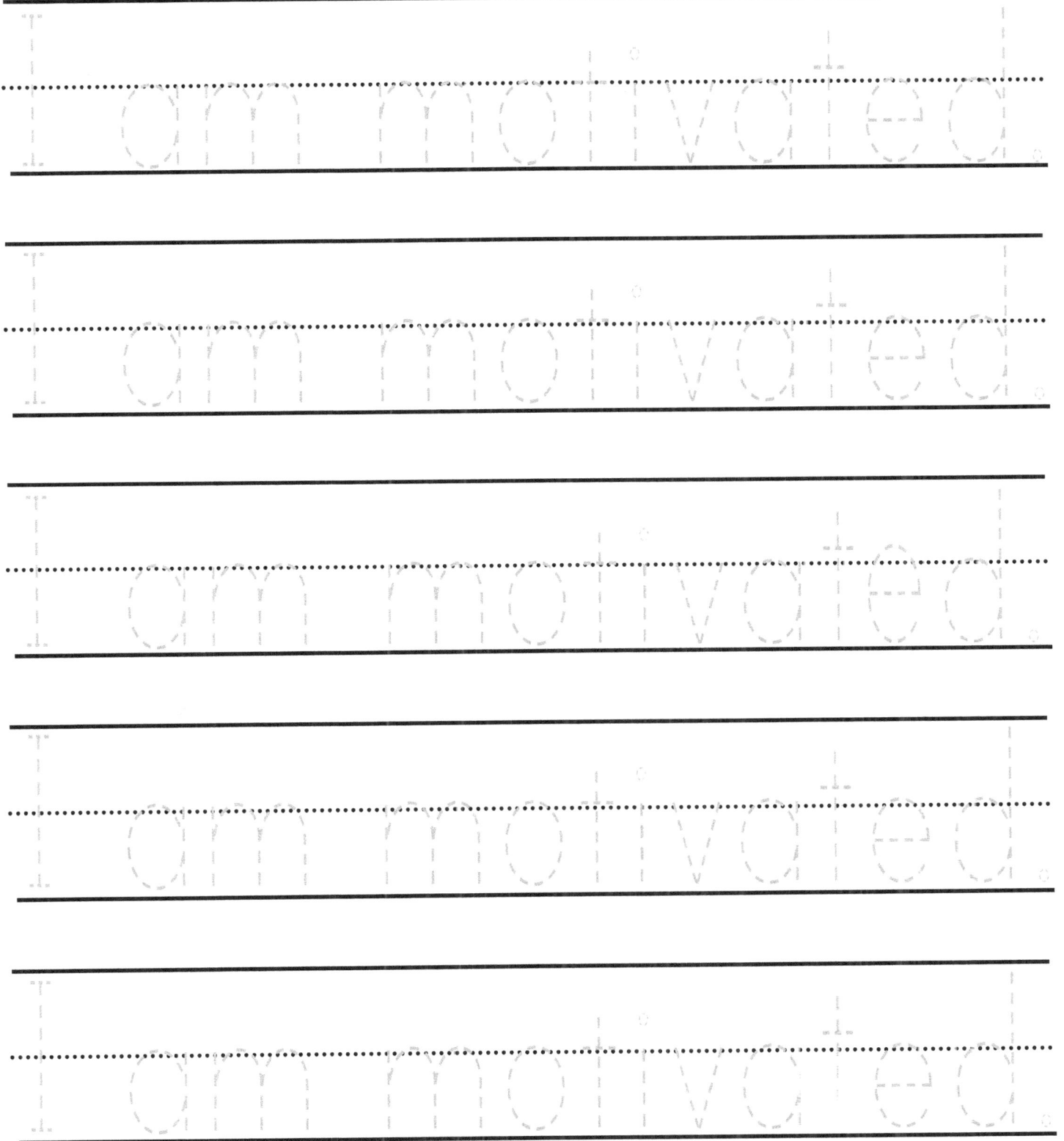

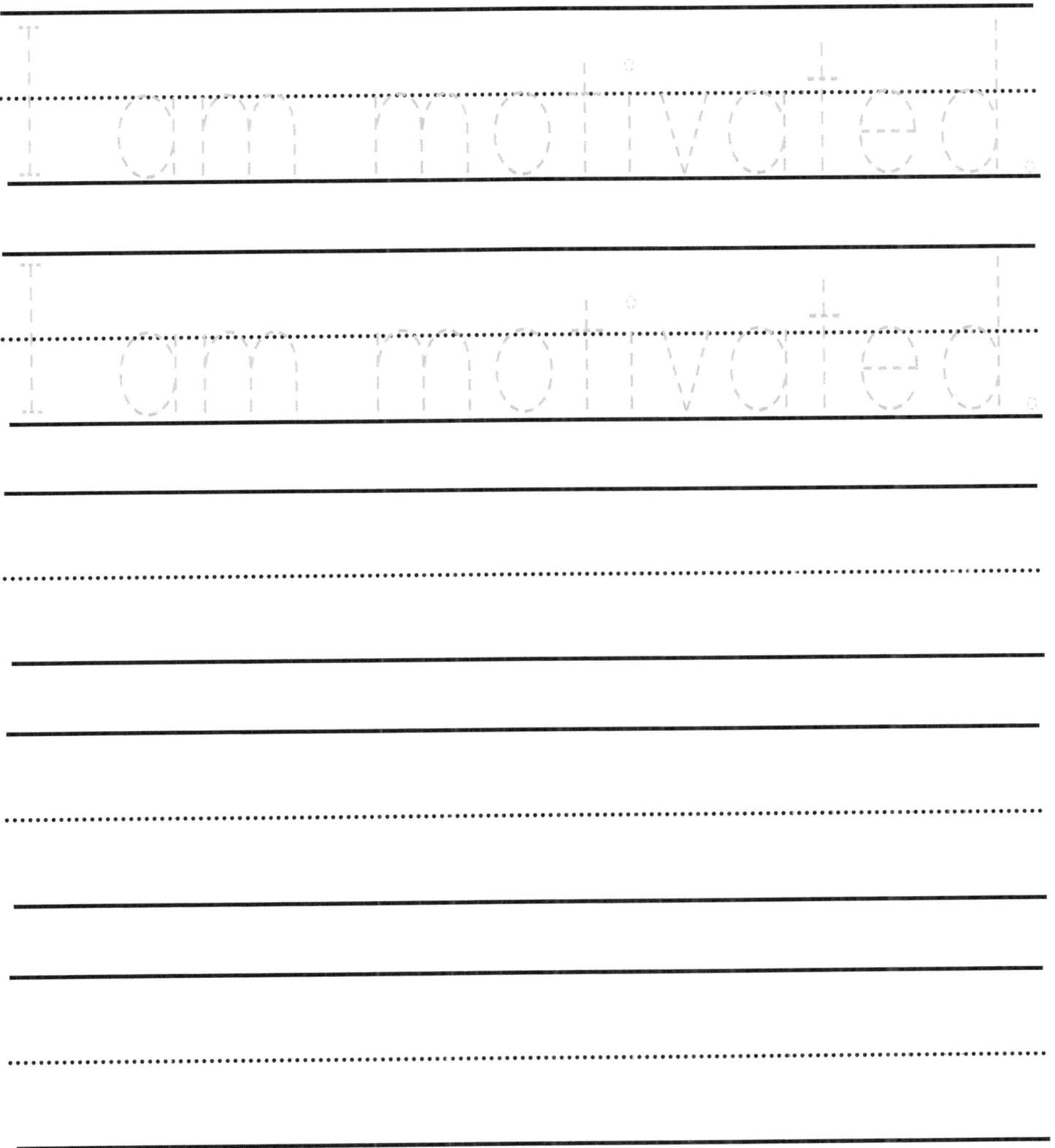

I am motivated.

I am motivated.

I AM NEEDED.

I AM LOVED.

I AM IMPORTANT.

My family and friends want me around.

N

Practice writing the affirmation in the lines below.

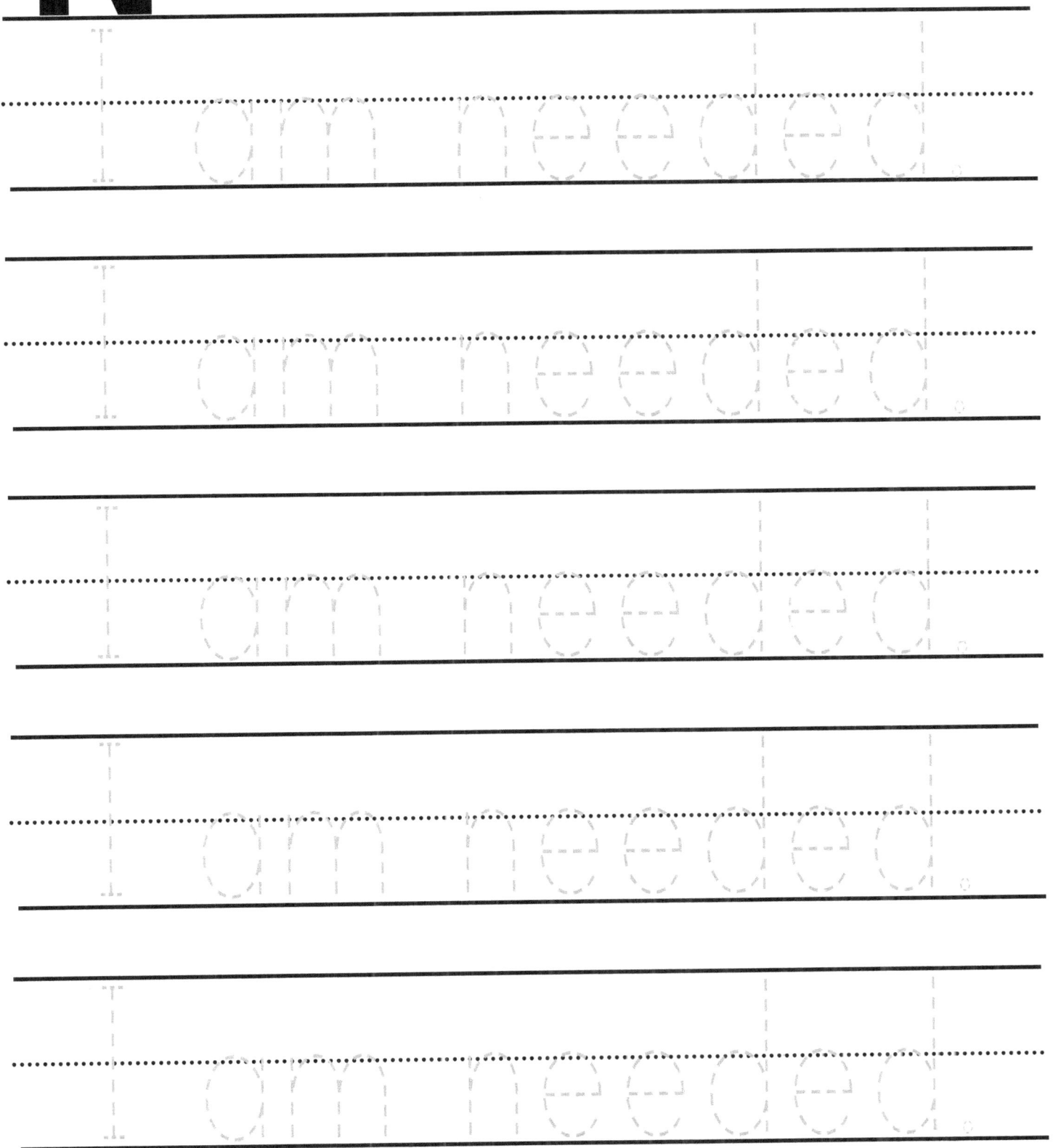

I am needed.

I am needed.

I am needed.

I am needed.

I am needed.

I am needed.

I am needed.

I AM OPTIMISTIC.

I FOCUS ON THE GOOD.

MY MIND IS POSITIVE.

Practice writing the affirmation in the lines below.

I am optimistic

I am optimistic

I am optimistic

I am optimistic

I am optimistic

I am optimistic

I am optimistic

I AM POWERFUL.

I HAVE ENDLESS POTENTIAL.

I HAVE THE POWER TO MAKE MY DREAMS COME TRUE.

P

Practice writing the affirmation in the lines below.

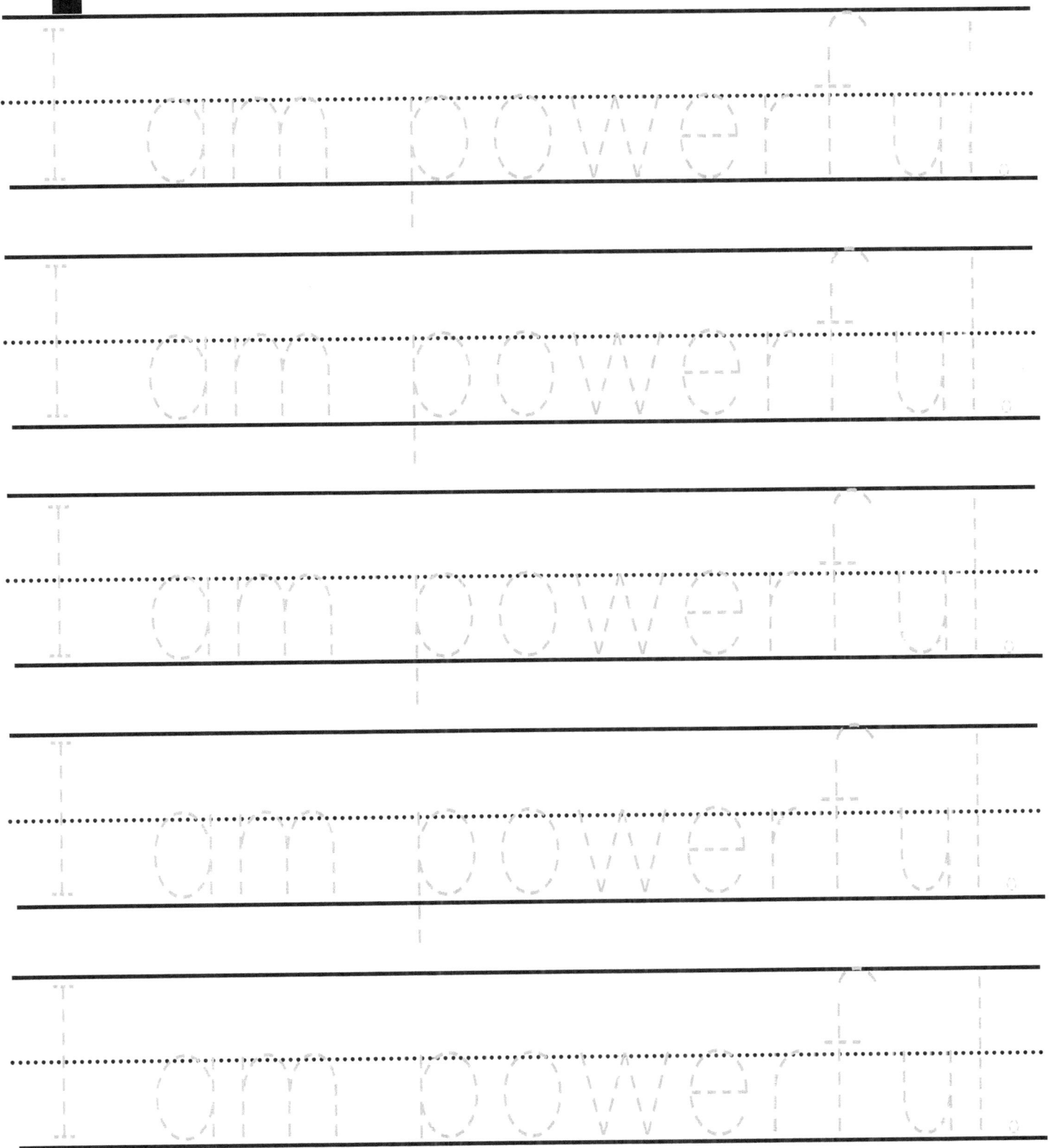

Q

Practice writing the affirmation in the lines below.

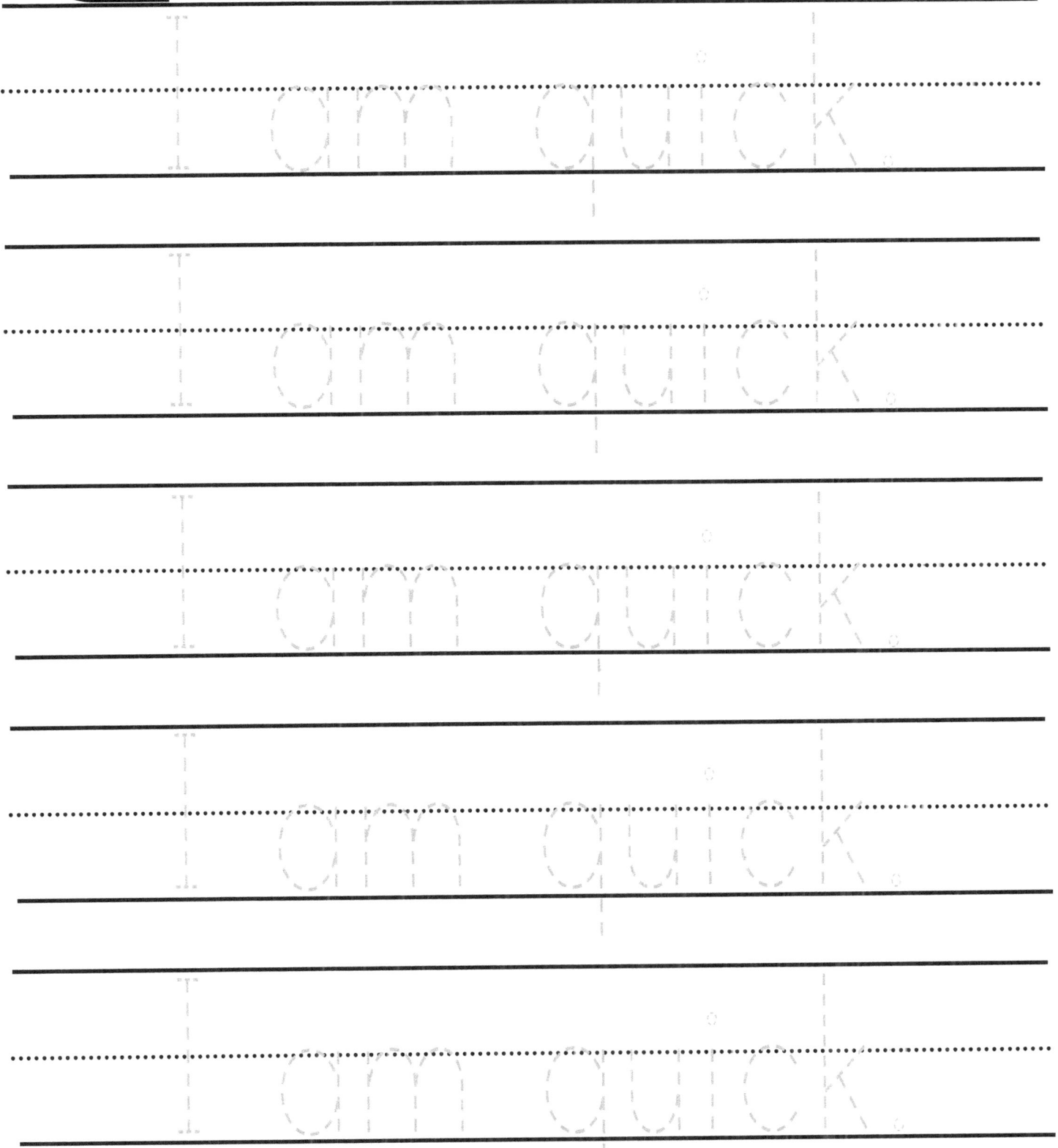

I am quick.

R

Practice writing the affirmation in the lines below.

I show respect

I show respect

I show respect

I show respect

I show respect

I show respect

I show respect

S

Practice writing the affirmation in the lines below.

I am strong

I am strong

I AM TALENTED.
I AM GOOD AT MANY THINGS.

T

Practice writing the affirmation in the lines below.

I am talented

I am talented

I am talented

I am talented

I am talented

I am talented.

I am talented.

U

Practice writing the affirmation in the lines below.

I am unique

I am unique

MY VOICE MATTERS.

WHAT I SAY IS IMPORTANT.

V

Practice writing the affirmation in the lines below.

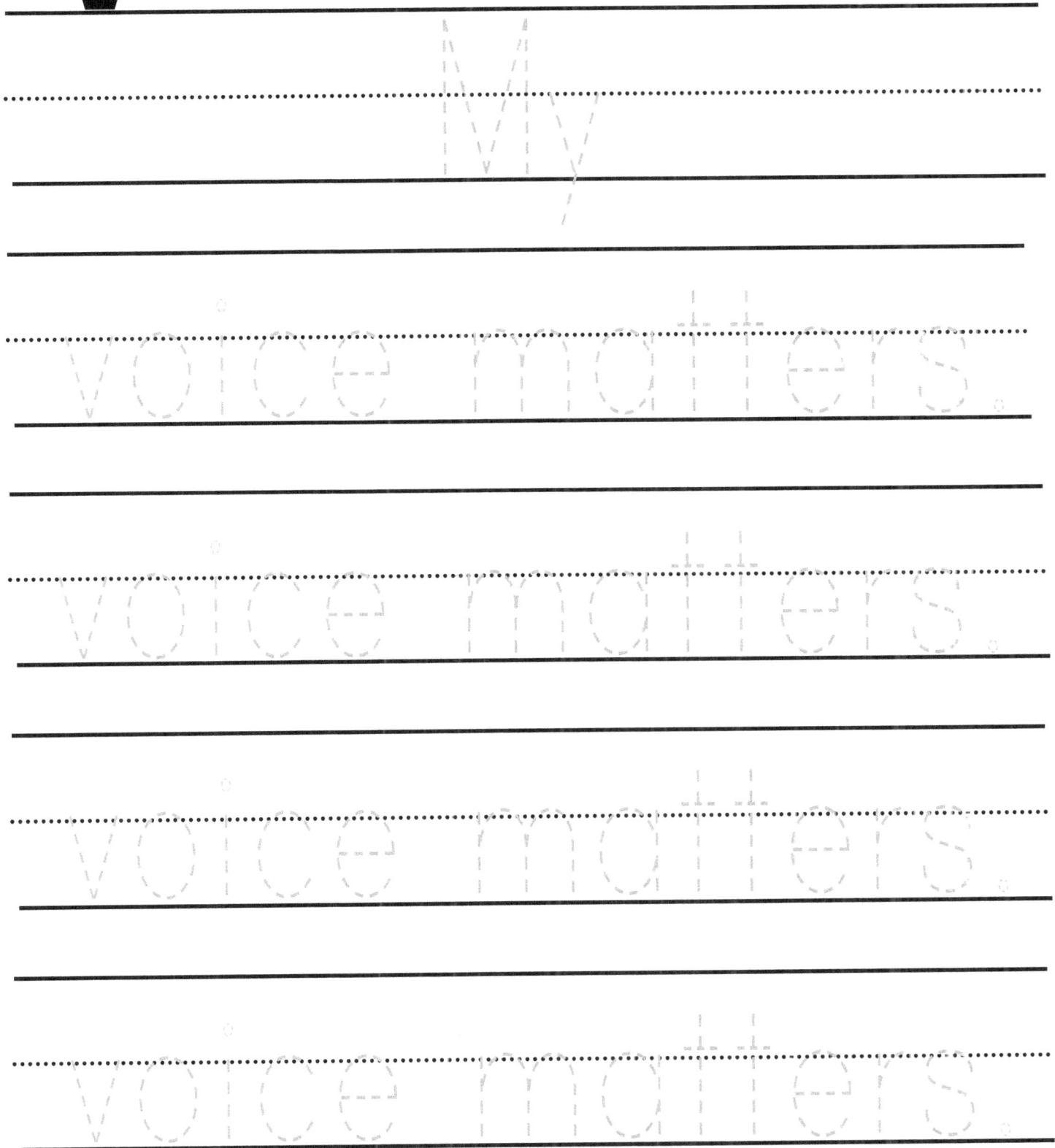

My voice matters. voice matters. voice matters. voice matters.

voice matters.

voice matters.

I AM A WINNER

I AM A WINNER.

I ALWAYS TRY MY BEST.

I WILL NOT QUIT.

W Practice writing the affirmation in the lines below.

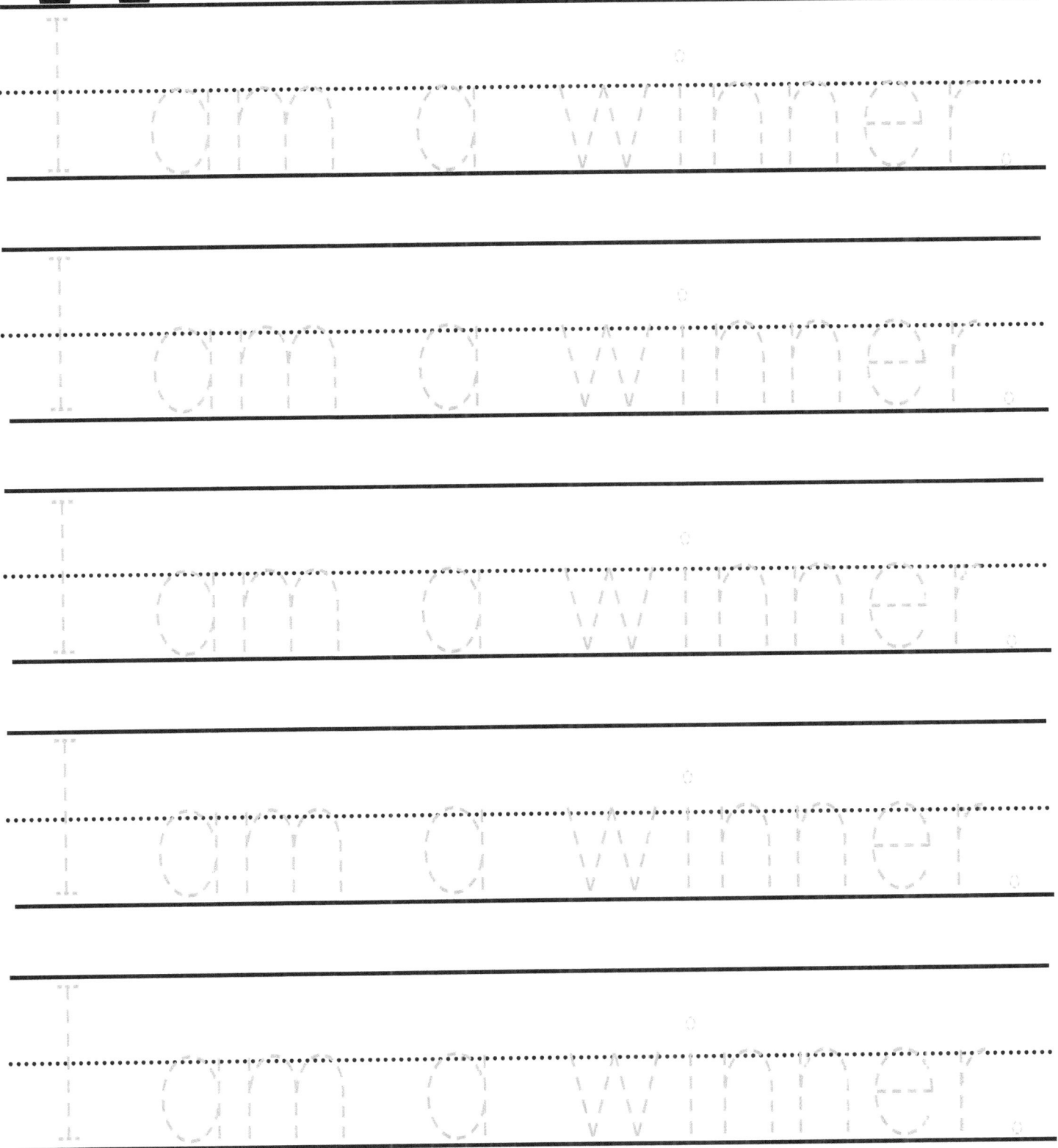

I am a winner

I am a winner

I am a winner

I am a winner

I am a winner

I am a winner

I am a winner

I AM EXCEPTIONAL.

I IMPROVE EVERYDAY.

EVERY PROBLEM HAS A SOLUTION.

Practice writing the affirmation in the lines below.

I am exceptional.

I am exceptional.

I am exceptional.

I am exceptional.

I am exceptional.

I am exceptional.

I am exceptional.

I SAY YES TO NEW THINGS

Y

Practice writing the affirmation in the lines below.

I say

yes to new things

yes to new things

yes to new things

yes to new things

yes to new things

yes to new things

Z

Practice writing the affirmation in the lines below.

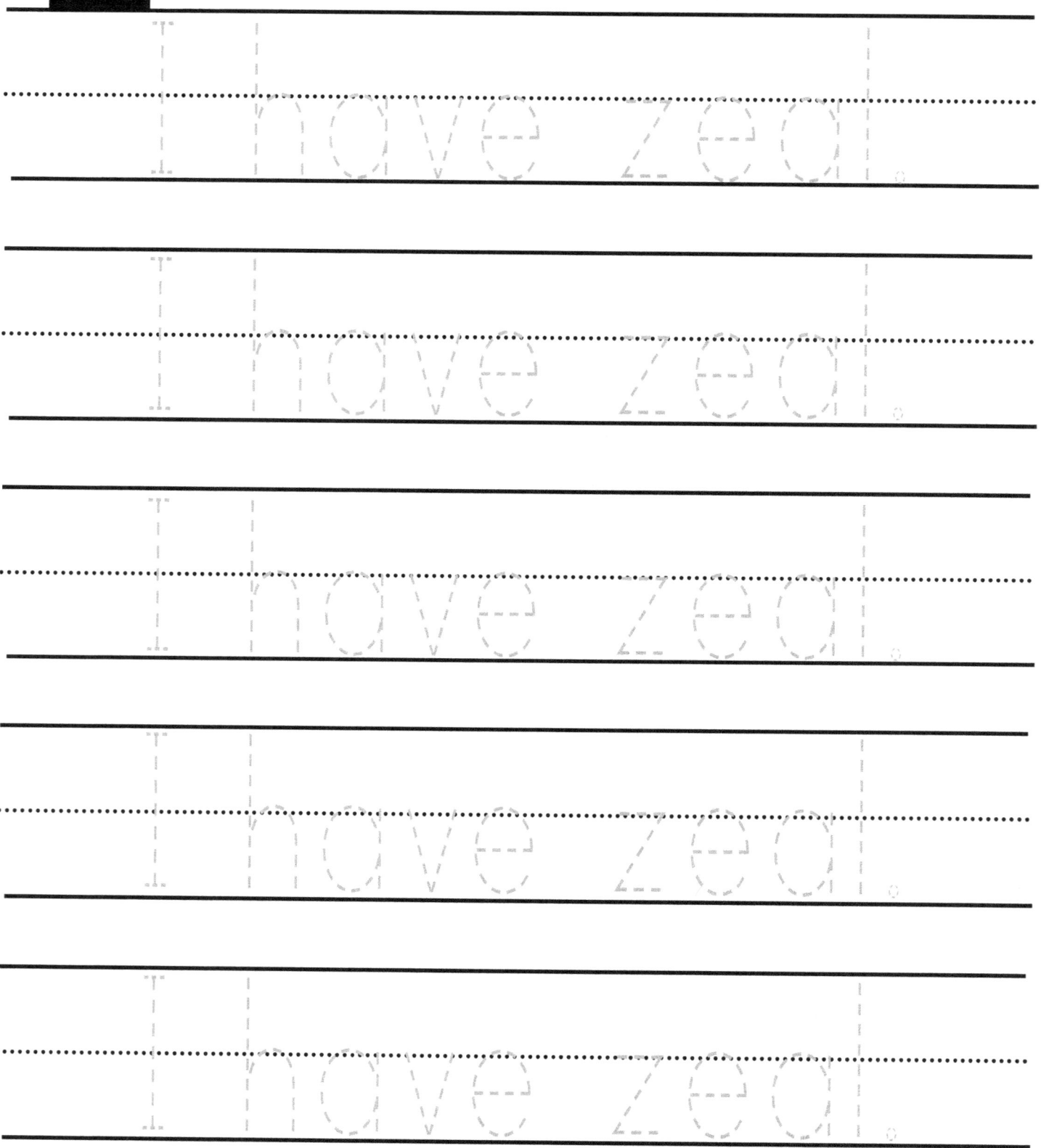

I have zeal.

I have zeal.

I have zeal.

I have zeal.

I have zeal.

I have zeal.

I have zeal.

HOW TO BUILD AN AFFIRMATION LIST

 **FILL IN THE BLANK WITH CHILD'S NAME.**

 **USE POSITIVE WORDS.**

 **WRITE IN PRESENT TENSE.**

 **KEEP IT SHORT AND TO THE POINT.**

 **CUT OUT AND STORE SOMEWHERE TO SEE EVERYDAY.**

 **PRACTICE SAYING THE AFFIRMATIONS EVERYDAY.**

_____ 's

AFFIRMATIONS

START WITH: :....: I AM :....: OR :....: I CAN :....:

1

2

3

4

5

My Alphabet Affirmations
by Black Blossom Press